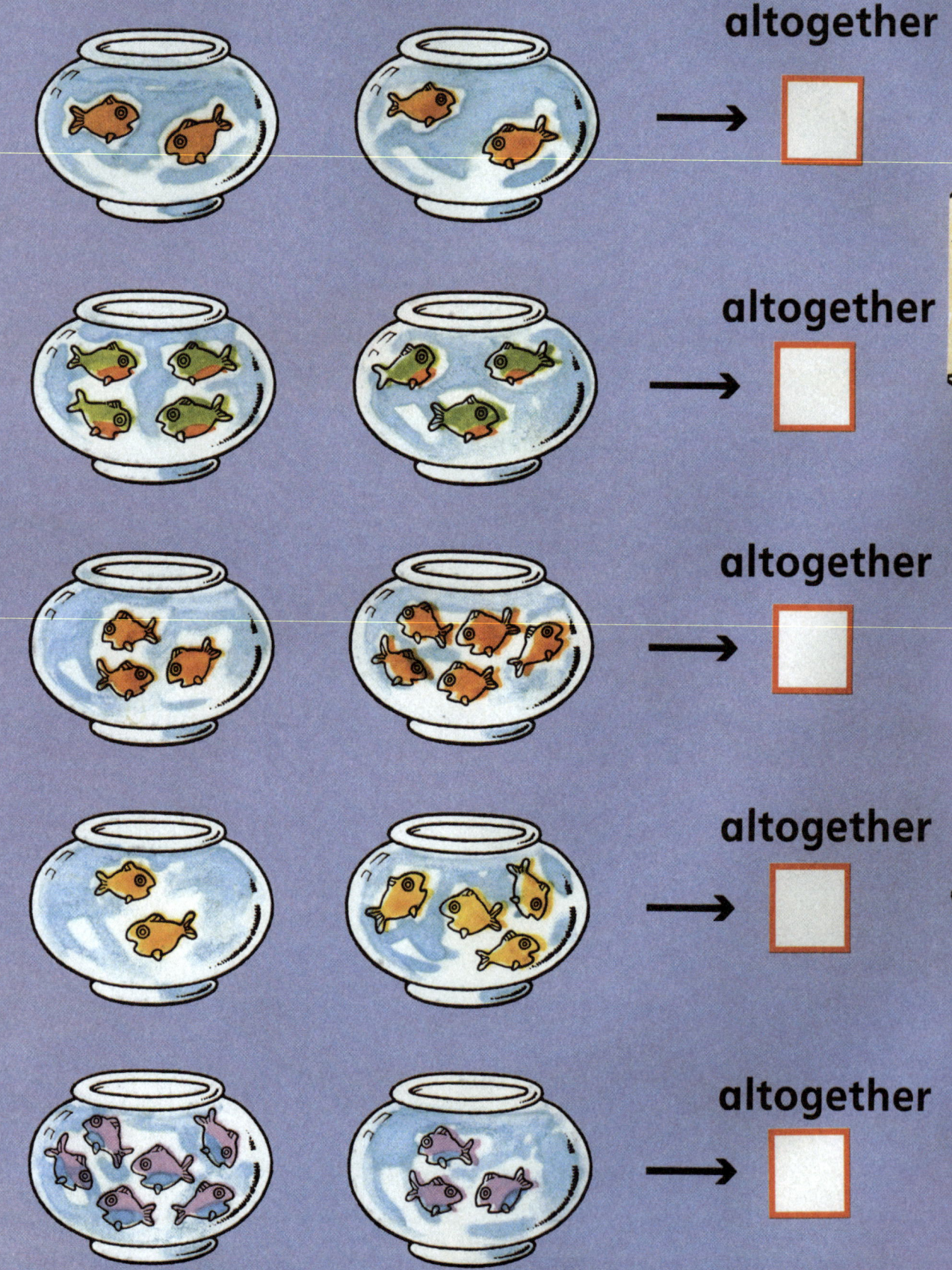

Concept of addition

Put fish in the jars.

2 and 1 ⟶ ☐

1 and 3 ⟶ ☐

3 and 2 ⟶ ☐

4 and 2 ⟶ ☐

3 and 3 ⟶ ☐

Concept of addition

Girls and boys

Put in

5 girls	2 boys	→ ☐ altogether
5 girls	5 boys	→ ☐ altogether
3 girls	6 boys	→ ☐ altogether
2 girls	6 boys	→ ☐ altogether

Girls and boys

Concept of addition

4

3 and 3 →

and →

and →

and →

and →

and →

Concept of addition

Draw and add.

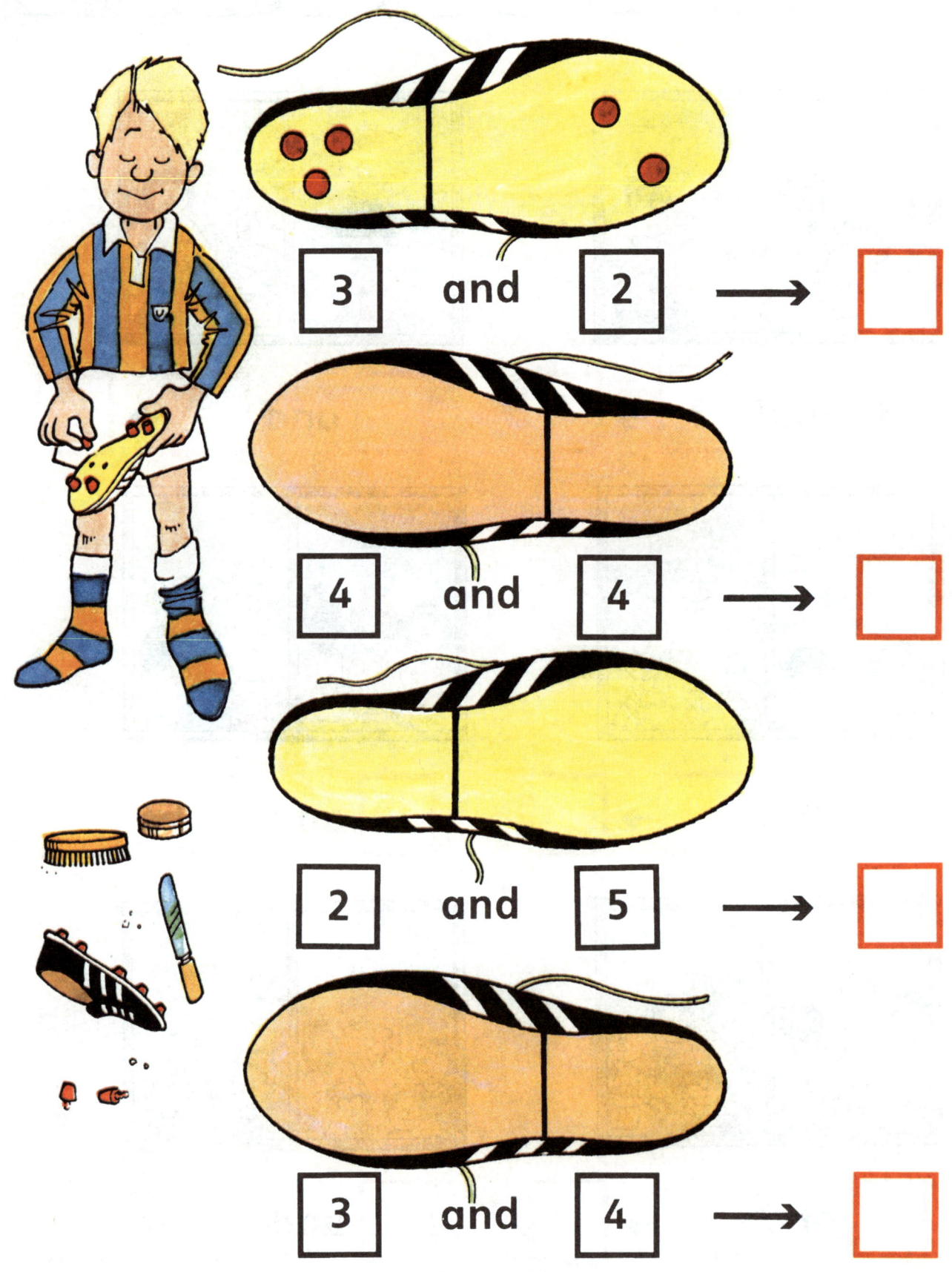

3 and 2 →

4 and 4 →

2 and 5 →

3 and 4 →

How many altogether?

Adding on 1

Peas

1 add 1 → 2
2 add 1 →
3 add 1 →
4 add 1 →
5 add 1 →
6 add 1 →
7 add 1 →
8 add 1 →
9 add 1 →

Adding on 2

8

Ice cubes

Put in 6 .
Add 2.

6 add 2 → ☐

Put in 3 .
Add 2.

3 add 2 → ☐

1 add 2 → ☐   5 add 2 → ☐

2 add 2 → ☐   6 add 2 → ☐

3 add 2 → ☐   7 add 2 → ☐

4 add 2 → ☐   8 add 2 → ☐

R1

Adding 1 or 2

Adding 1 or 2

3 + 1 → ☐

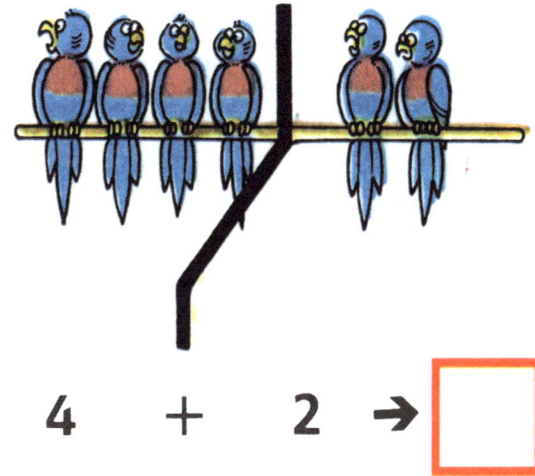

4 + 2 → ☐

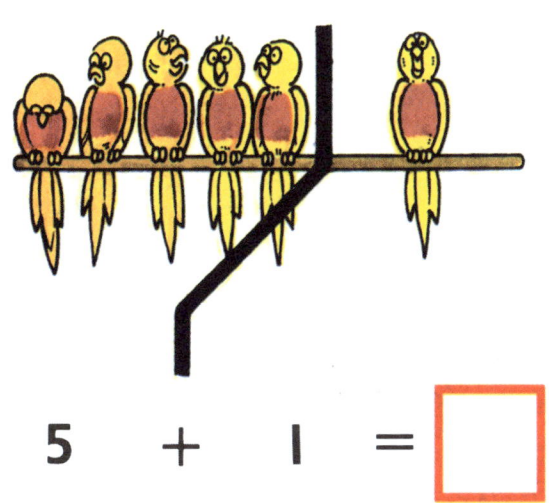

5 + 1 = ☐

2 + ☐ = ☐

☐ + ☐ = ☐

☐ + ☐ = ☐

Totals of 4   Investigation

Put 4 spots on the monster.

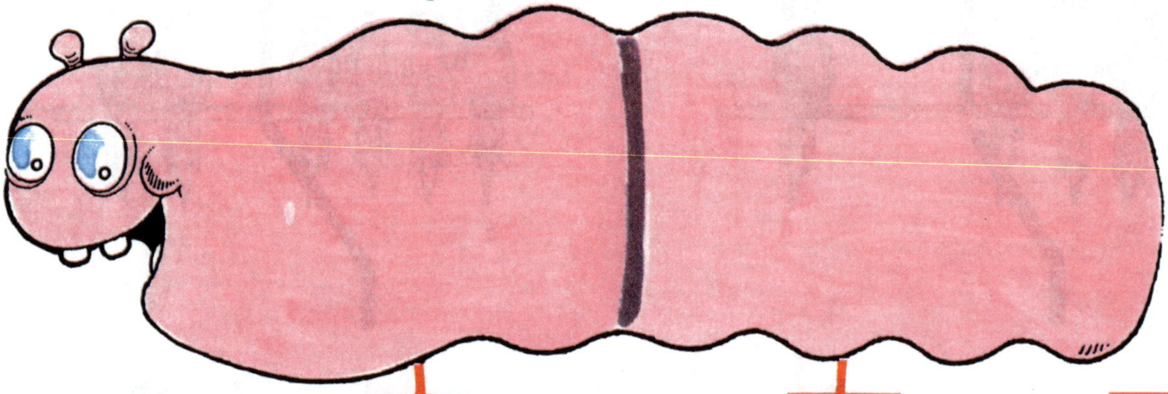

☐ + ☐ = 4

☐ + ☐ = 4

☐ + ☐ = 4

☐ + ☐ + ☐ = 4

☐ + ☐ + ☐ = 4

☐ + ☐ + ☐ = 4

Totals to 4

12

Draw spots.

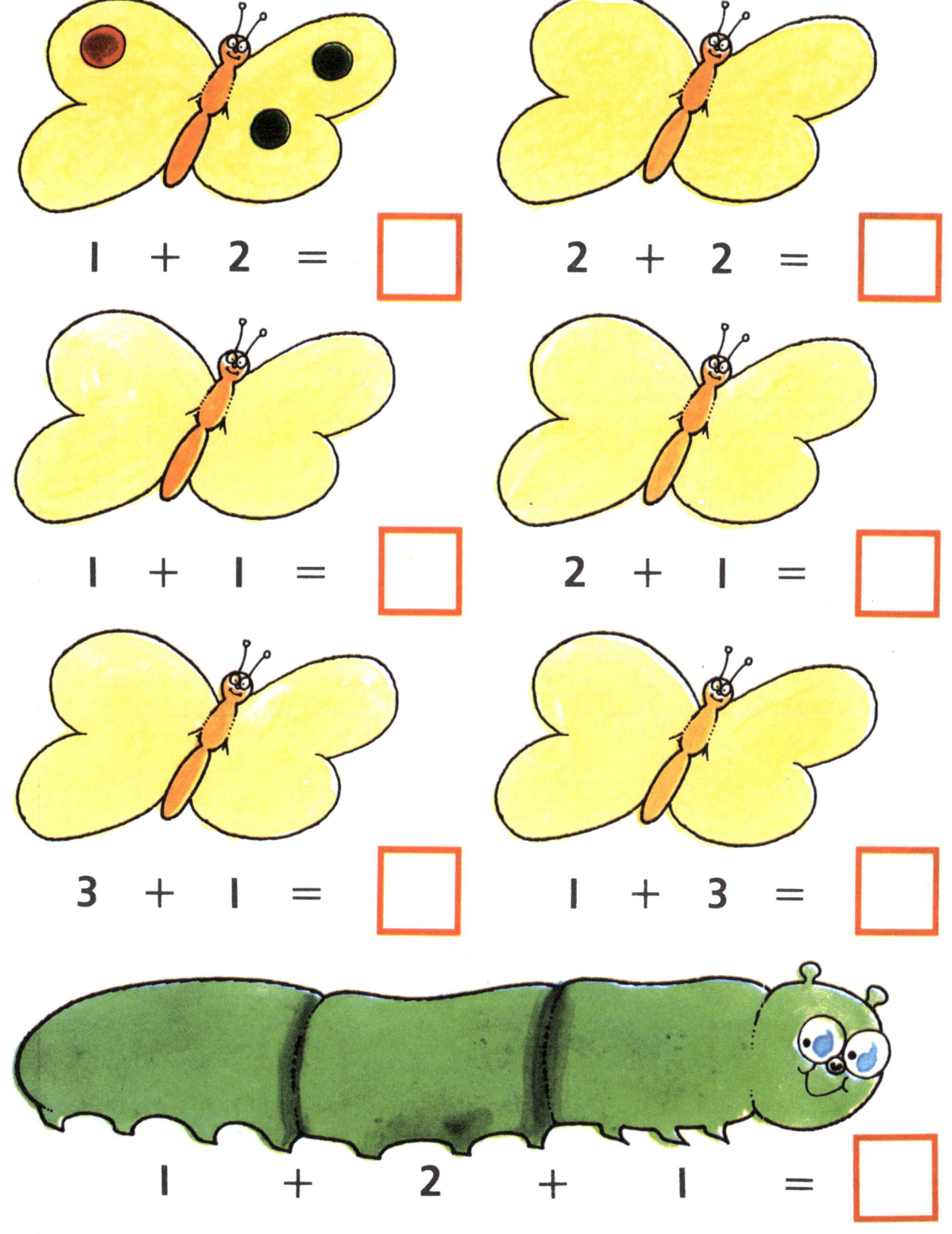

1 + 2 = ☐   2 + 2 = ☐

1 + 1 = ☐   2 + 1 = ☐

3 + 1 = ☐   1 + 3 = ☐

1 + 2 + 1 = ☐

Put in 5 parcels.

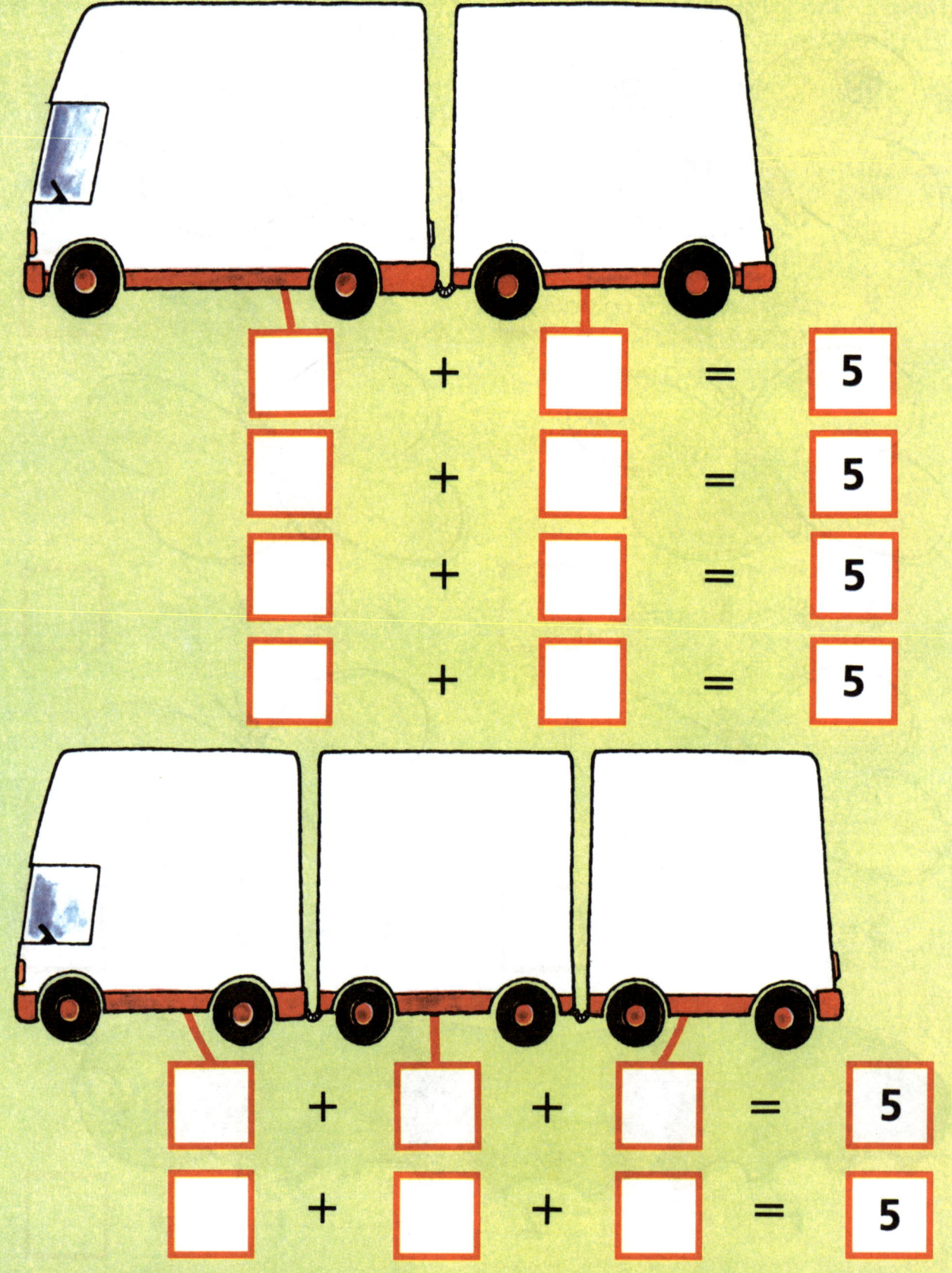

Totals to 5

Draw and add.

3 + 1 = ☐

4 + 1 = ☐

3 + 2 = ☐

2 + 3 = ☐

2 + 2 = ☐

1 + 4 = ☐

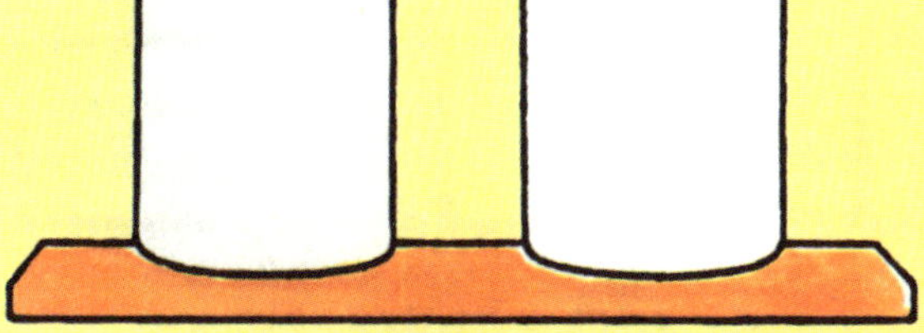

1 + 3 = ☐

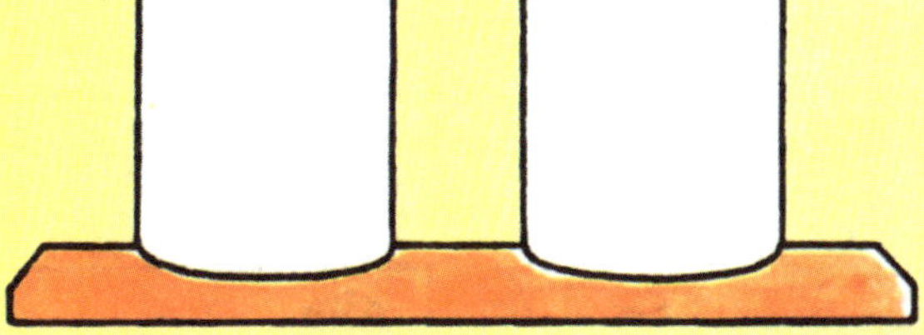

2 + 3 = ☐

Totals of 5

Count and add.

Spots

Monday

1 + 5 = 6

Tuesday

2 + 4 =

Wednesday

3 +

Thursday

Friday

Saturday

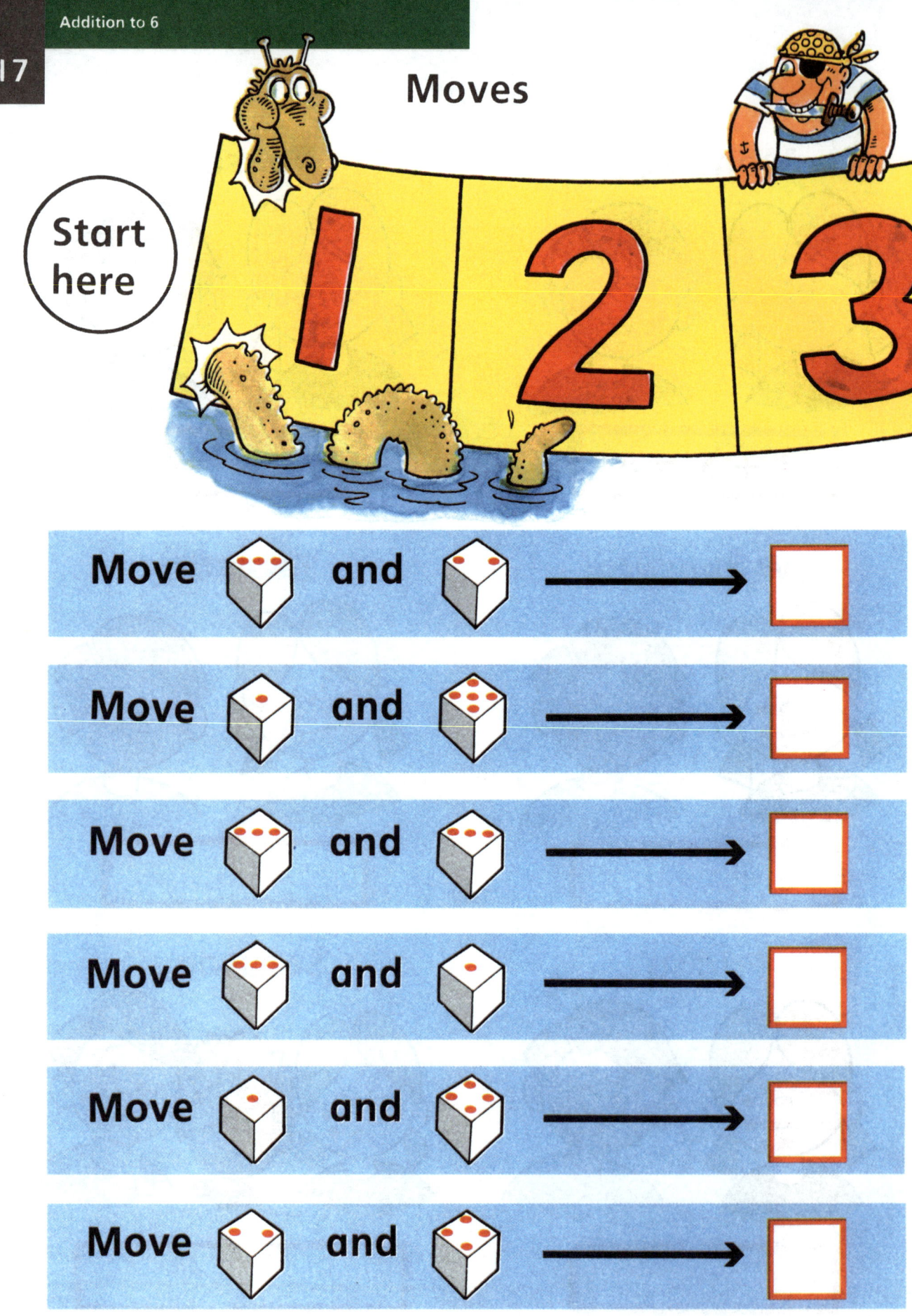

Addition to 6

18

4 + 1 =

Extension

Draw dots.

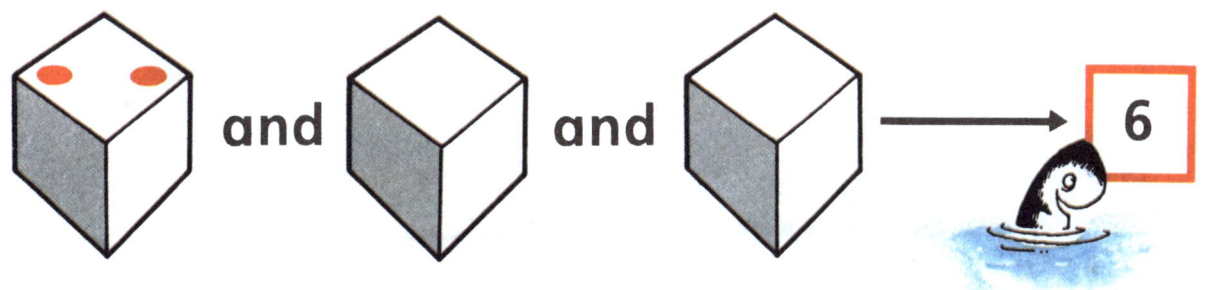 and and → 6

Addition to 6p

Buy  1p and 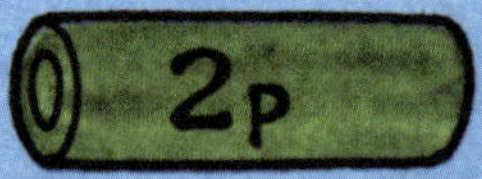 2p ☐

Buy 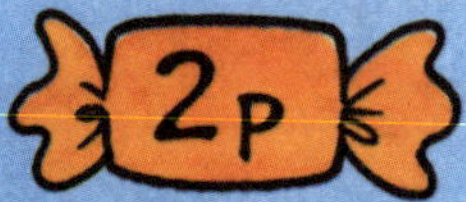 2p and  3p ☐

Buy  3p and  3p ☐

Buy  1p and  2p ☐

Buy  3p and 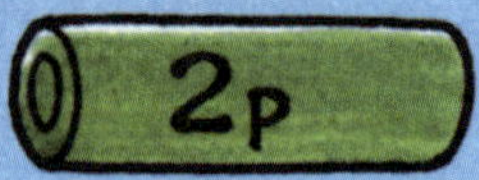 2p ☐

Buy 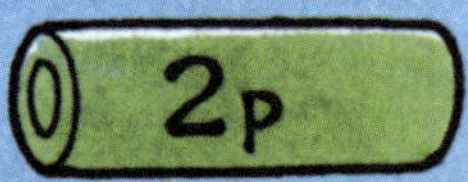 2p and 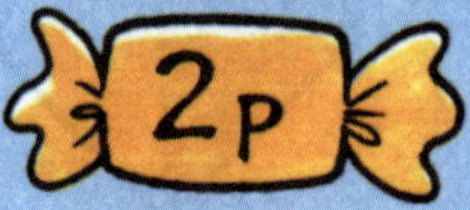 2p ☐

Addition to 6p

Make each 1p more.

- 1p → 2p
- 4p →
- 2p →
- 3p →

Make each 2p more.

- 2p →
- 3p →
- 4p →
- 1p →

Pets

2 + 1 =

1 + 2 =

3 + 1 =

1 + 3 =

4 + 1 =

1 + 4 =

3 + 2 =

2 + 3 =

5 + 1 =

1 + 5 =

4 + 2 =

2 + 4 =

How many?

on the bridge ☐

under the bridge ☐

altogether ☐

on the branch ☐

under the branch ☐

altogether ☐

on the rope ☐

under the rope ☐

altogether ☐

on the desk ☐

under the desk ☐

altogether ☐

Addition to 6 — **Extension**

Fish

Write number stories 🐟 2 + 3 = 5

🐟	⭐
🐟	🐟
🦀	🐙